"*About the noblest work that man can do is the developmen continent of yours.*"—THOMAS HUGHES, M.

292

# The New Northwest:

AN

# ADDRESS

BY

# HON. WM. D. KELLEY

[Reported by D. WOLFE BROWN, Phonographer.]

ON THE

# NORTHERN PACIFIC RAILWAY,

IN ITS RELATIONS TO THE DEVELOPMENT OF THE NORTHWESTERN SECTION OF THE UNITED STATES, AND TO THE INDUSTRIAL AND COMMERCIAL INTERESTS OF THE NATION.

# Correspondence.

Philadelphia, May 27th, 1871.

*HON. WILLIAM D. KELLEY:*

Dear Sir:—Recognizing your position as a representative American, with an intelligent interest in the material progress of the country, we respectfully ask you to address the Commercial Exchange and the citizens of Philadelphia, at your earliest convenience, on the development of the Northwest section of the Continent by the building of the Northern Pacific Railroad, and the effect of this enterprise upon the trade, manufactures and commerce of our State and city.

Very respectfully, your obedient servants,

S. I. Comly,
*President Commercial Exchange.*
Morton McMichael,
M. Baird & Co.,
E. Harper Jeffries,
George L. Buzby,
S. J. Christian,
Samuel M. Felton,
*President Pennsylvania Steel Co.*
Washington J. Jackson,
P. A. Keller,
Herman J. Lombaert,
*President American Steamship Co.*
J. W. Jones,
*Sec. Philadelphia and Reading Railroad.*
Thomas A. Scott,
*Pres. Pa. Co. and P. C. and S. L. R. R.*
J. G. Fell,
A. R. McHenry,
Lewis Audenreid,
Edwin N. Benson,
John P. Wetherill,
A. Whitney & Sons,
C. H. Clark,
James L. Claghorn,
G. M. Troutman,
Asa Packer,
*President Lehigh Valley Railroad.*
E. A. Rollins,
N. B. Browne,
Thomas Robins,
John Jordan, Jr.,
Henry H. Bingham,
Alex. G. Cattell & Co.,
Dell Noblit, Jr.,
Logan Bros. & Co.,
Frederick Fraley,
J. Edgar Thomson,
*President Pennsylvania Railroad.*
Thomas Smith,
Henry D. Welsh,
Henry Lewis,
Daniel Smith, Jr.,
William G. Crowell,
J. W. Forney,
William C. Longstreth,
Coffin Colket,
Charles Platt,
Isaac Hinckley,
*President P. W. and B. Railroad.*
W. W. Harding,
George H. Stuart,
A. P. Colesbury,
D. Faust,
Joel J. Baily & Co.,
John O. James,
Charles Santee,
Samuel H. Shipley,
Thomas C. Hand,
D. B. Cummins,
Arthur G. Coffin,
Henry D. Sherrerd,
J. P. Aertsen,
*Treas. H. and B. T. M. R. R. and Coal Co.*
M. P. Hutchinson,
*President Catawissa Railroad.*
W. L. Gilroy,
*Treasurer Catawissa Railroad.*
F. A. Comly,
*President North Pennsylvania Railroad.*
G. A. Wood,
E. C. Knight & Co.,
R. H. Downing,
*President B. and S. R. R. Co.*

Philadelphia, June 5th, 1871.

GENTLEMEN:—Your invitation to address the citizens of Philadelphia on the development of the Northwestern section of the United States by the building of the Northern Pacific Railroad, and the effect of this enterprise upon the trade, manufactures and commerce of our State and city, invites me to continue in the advocacy of an enterprise for the promotion of which I have, as opportunity offered, labored for more than a quarter of a century.

I will find pleasure in complying with your request on the evening of Monday next, the 12th inst. With thanks for the flattering terms in which you were pleased to express your wishes, I am,

Very truly yours,

WILLIAM D. KELLEY.

To S. I. Comly, J. Edgar Thomson, Thomas A. Scott, John O. James, M. Baird & Co., George H. Stuart, and others.

---

The public meeting, which was called in pursuance of the above correspondence, assembled in the American Academy of Music, on the evening of Monday, June 12. A crowded audience of more than four thousand citizens of Philadelphia, and prominent gentlemen from other parts of Pennsylvania, attested the general interest felt in the subject to be discussed.

The meeting was called to order by Seth I. Comly, Esq., and the following officers were then elected:

*President:*

HIS EXCELLENCY JOHN W. GEARY,
GOVERNOR OF PENNSYLVANIA.

*Vice-Presidents:*

Hon. JOHN SWIFT,
Col. JAMES PAGE,
WM. M. MEREDITH,
J. O. JAMES,
A. J. LEWIS,
JOS. PRICE,
HENRY M. PHILLIPS,
JOHN FARNUM,
NATHAN BROOKE,
WASH. J. JACKSON,
GEORGE FALES,
JOHN SELLERS,
HENRY WINSOR,
MATTHEW BAIRD,
Gen. R. PATTERSON,
ALEXANDER BROWN,
Gen. W. MCCANDLESS,
Gen. H. H. BINGHAM,
A. G. CATTELL,
ROBT. P. DECHERT,
A. J. DERBYSHIRE,
JAY COOKE,
S. BRADFORD,
RICHARD WRIGHT,
JOHN A. HOUSEMAN,
HENRY C. CAREY,
HENRY G. MORRIS,
J. RINALDO SANK,
JAMES MCMANES,
C. A. GRISCOM,
CHARLES WHEELER,
J. H. MICHENER,
JAMES C. HAND,
ALEX. WHILLDIN,
SETH I. COMLY,
N. B. BROWNE,
WILLIAM MASSEY,
FURMAN SHEPPARD,
S. A. CROZER,
WM. B. BEMENT,
WM. GILLESPIE,
MORTON MCMICHAEL,
ALFRED DAY,
WILLIAM ELLIOTT,
CALEB COPE,
GEORGE A. WOOD,
WM. V. MCGRATH,
MORRIS DAVIS,
JAMES POLLOCK,
SAML. J. REEVES,
SAML. E. STOKES,
E. Y. TOWNSEND,
JACOB RIEGEL,
THOS. E. HAND,
EVAN RANDOLPH,
ISAAC JEANES,
LEWIS AUDENREID,
E. H. TROTTER,
JAS. F. STOCKDALE,
BENJAMIN BULLOCK,
HENRY PREAUT,
CLARENCE H. CLARKE,
JOHN DEVEREUX,
B. K. JAMISON,
WILLIAM GREER,
FRED. H. NEWHALL,
HENRY C. GIBSON,
JOSIAH BACON,
DR. E. C. KAMERLY,
GEO. L. HARRISON,
JAMES ALBRIGHT,
GEORGE WHITNEY,
E. W. CLARKE,
E. A. KNIGHT,
J. GILLINGHAM FELL,
GEORGE G. PARRISH,

J. G. Rosengarten,
John C. McCall,
William S. Grant,
William D. Lewis,
Gen. C. M. Prevost,
George W. Biddle,
E. C. Knight,
J. B. Lippincott,
Coffin Colket,
Wm. H. Horstmann,
E. Harper Jeffries,
Alfred D. Jessup,
David S. Brown,
Joseph Lea,
Francis R. Cope,
Andrew Wheeler,
William J. Nead,
John J. Thompson,
Thomas Smith,
D. B. Cummins,
E. M. Lewis,
B. B. Comegys,
Joseph Moore,
A. G. Coffin,
William Adamson,
C. H. Schœner,
W. C. Allison,
J. B. McCreary,
Louis Wagner,
John E. Graeff,
Gen. Joshua T. Owen,
William Bumm,
Henry Lewis,
Richard Wood,
Samuel W. Cattell,
Henry Huhn,
James L. Claghorn,
John W. Forney,
Fred. Fraley,
W. W. Harding,
A. R. McHenry,
H. G. Gowen,
Robert Shoemaker,
Charles Vezin,
F. W. Lockwood,
L. Westergaard,
Jos. Bailey,
J. E. Caldwell,
J. M. Whitall,
H. B. Benners,
L. C. Madeira,
Thomas B. Wattson,
William Brockie,
George C. Carson,
C. P. Knight,
John L. Hough,
P. B. Mingle,
Fred. Gerker,
E. C. Eby,
William B. Mann,
James Graham,
H. W. Workman,
Jerry Walker,
E. A. Souder,
William Cummings,
Theo. Cuyler,
Robert K. Neff,

G. F. Lennig,
Gen. Robt. L. Bodine,
J. Edgar Thomson,
A. C. Craige,
Stephen Flanagan,
B. H. Bartel,
Thomas Clyde,
J. Vaughn Merrick,
Henry Geiger,
A. J. Focht,
Ed. S. Handy,
Wm. McAleer,
J. S. Newlin,
Benj. Horner,
Charles J. Sharpless,
Reeve L. Knight,
Clement Biddle,
Benj. Orne,
John W. Thomas,
Henry M. Stone,
C. H. Cummings,
W. E. Lockwood,
Madison R. Harris,
Charles Smith,
P. S. Janney,
Francis Jordan,
J. V. Creely,
Isaac G. Colesberry,
Hon. J. F. Belsterling,
Charles B. Trego,
N. P. Shortridge,
H. H. Lippincott,
John H. Krause,
Thornton Conrow,
Jas. S. Martin,
George J. Waterman,
William T. Kirk,
Isaac Hough,
F. F. Bernadou,
William L. James,
Henry Marcus,
C. H. Garden,
Augustus Heaton,
William H. Sowers,
William S. Stokley,
John L. Shoemaker,
Thomas A. Scott,
J. M. Vance,
N. B. Kneass,
A. H. Franciscus,
E. P. Kershow,
E. Tracy,
Henry Davis,
Asa Whitney,
Wm. L. McDowell,
Henry D. Welsh,
A. F. Chesebrough,
E. H. Butler,
W. H. Flitcraft,
Henry W. Gray,
Isaac Kohn,
C. Magargee,
Robert H. Beatty,
J. M. Wilcox,
Samuel G. King,
Thomas Sparks,
George Truman,

M. J. Dohan,
Isaac Hinckley,
Thos. Dolan,
Herman J. Lombaert,
John P. Wetherill,
J. W. Jones,
Geo. A. Nicolls,
J. P. Aertsen,
M. P. Hutchinson,
Asa Packer,
E. A. Rollins,
F. A. Comly,
Geo. Howell,
Samuel Field,
Samuel Welsh,
John Welsh, Jr.,
John P. Verree,
Wm. E. Littleton,
Washington Butcher,
William Dorsey,
A. T. Eberman,
Robert Cornelius,
Samuel J. Christian,
William B. Ellison,
Thomas H. Moore,
A. K. McClure,
Peter Williamson,
Frederick Ladner,
J. L. Erringer,
William G. Boulton,
Edward S. Clarke,
Robert Toland,
William M. Greiner,
Edwin Greble,
William M. Baird,
John Rice,
Samuel T. Bodine,
William Purves,
Saunders Lewis,
Wm. C. Houston,
Joshua P. Eyre.
Thos. P. Stotesbury,
Daniel Smith,
Christian Hoffman,
Chas. Macalester,
Geo. H. Stuart,
Chas. S. Lewis,
John B. Austin,
Samuel Bispham,
Wm. Stevenson,
Samuel B. Thomas,
P. Fitzpatrick,
Moro Philips,
Jesse Godley,
D. H. Kirkpatrick,
W. H. Ashhurst,
John Robbins,
M. Hall Stanton,
William Anspach,
Orlando Crease,
Wm. A. Porter,
Edmund L. Levy,
Gen. Gideon Clarke,
Wm. L. Hirst,
Henry Boraef,
Jas. Bonbright,

Benj. Homer,
Charles Platt,
C. B. Durborow,
F. A. Klemm,
S. Gross Fry,
J. Fraley Smith,
Jos. H. Trotter,
Wm. Cramp,
L. C. Cassidy,
Geo. N. Allen,
John A. Shermer,
Louis Haehnlen,
Jacob G. Neafie,
Joseph Wayne,
Gen. John F. Ballier,
Alex M. Fox,
Jos. F. Marcer,
John O'Byrne,
Thos. G. Hood,
Thos. W. Evans,
Wm. R. Leeds,
George K. Zeigler,
D. C. W. Smith,
Wistar Morris,
Jno. H. Catherwood,
E. N. Benson,
H. C. Kellog,
Jos. H. Dulles,
George De B. Keim,
Stephen S. Price,
W. J. Pollock,
Alexander Kerr,
S. Fulton,
S. S. Scattergood,
James Abbott,
John S. Weimer,
George L. Buzby,
John H. Dohnert,
Israel Peterson,
John A. Brown,
Ambrose White,
John Mason,
Gilles Dallett,
Richard Vaux,
Charles McKeon,
Richard Ludlow,
Thaddeus Fairbanks,
Arthur Colburn,
Wm. M. Wilson,
Paul Graff,
J. Harvey Cochran,
Alf. E. Harmer,
Leonard Myers,
Samuel J. Randall,
Wm. E. Miskey,
D. Landreth,
Richard Levick,
A. A. Shumway,
W. J. Caner,
John Wanamaker,
D. H. Rockhill,
T. S. Emery,
J. J. Buchey,
Thos. S. Fernon,
J. E. Addicks,
Henry D. Sherrerd.

*Secretaries:*

Alex. P. Colesberry,
George A. Smith,
Lorin Blodget,
Stephen N. Winslow,
Clayton McMichael,
Eli T. Starr,
Lewis Waln Smith,
Peter Lesley,
John D. Stockton,
Jas. S. Chambers,
Wm. F. Corbit,
Alex. J. McCleary,
Wm. H. Cunnington,
Wm. B. Hanna,
David F. Houston,
Albert Frick,
G. W. Hamersley,
Riter Fitzgerald,
Charles K. Ide,
George G. Pierie,
Harry Todd,
Frank Wells,
R. Shel. Mackenzie,
John D. Watson,
Jos. K. McCammon,
Chas. E. Warburton,
W. W. Nevin,
C. E. School,
E. E. Morwitz,
Jos. H. Paist,
Robt. A. Welsh,
Dennis F. Dealy,
Jas. B. Alexander,
E. J. Swartz,
Jos. Robinson,
Chas. McClintock,
F. W. Thomas,
Robt. Friedlande,
John Blakeley,
John G. Ford,
Edmund Deacon.

---

Governor Geary, on taking the chair, said:

Fellow Citizens:—Having been called to preside over the deliberations of this vast and intelligent assembly, I desire to return to you my most sincere thanks for such an honorable compliment.

We have met this evening, not for the purpose of rehearsing the oft-repeated stories of triumphant marches and victorious battle-fields, of squandered treasure and sacrificed human lives, but to hear and learn from the eloquent and distinguished gentlemen who will, in discussing one of the most important enterprises of the age, address us upon some of the most distinguishing physical features of our country, and in so doing illustrate its wonderful progress and material growth from the Atlantic to the Pacific ocean.

Particular reference will doubtless be made to the various resources and advantages of that portion of the United States territory to be traversed by the Northern Pacific Railroad, now in process of construction.

From the stern alarms of a recent civil war we turn with pleasure to the cultivation and advancement of all the arts of peace, and the development of the matchless resources of our country. It is our desire to keep pace with all the laws of progress in such manner as will guarantee life, liberty and the pursuit of happiness to all who may desire to seek new homes in the magnificent territory about to be developed, whether they be to the "manor born" or are "strangers within our gates," and thus prove that "Peace hath victories no less renowned than war."

Through the influence, wisdom and enterprise of some of the prominent merchants, bankers and railroad men of Pennsylvania, the Northern Pacific Railroad will receive and discharge many of it passengers and much of it valuable freight in Philadelphia. It will make our State the great thoroughfare of nations, and our steamship line to Europe will be an assured success.

Pennsylvanians, therefore, should not be indifferent to the Northern Pacific Railroad, as they have their highest interests involved in its prompt prosecution and speedy construction.

In conclusion, fellow citizens, I invoke your earnest co-operation and assistance in this great work, by which, in addition to the subservance of personal and local interests, the most distant portions of our country will not only be united and bound together with bonds of iron, but by the more indissoluble links of a common brotherhood. I have now the honor of introducing the orator of the evening, Hon. William D. Kelley.

# The Great Thoroughfare.

Hon. WILLIAM D. KELLEY, who was received with hearty and long-continued applause, said:

I thank you, ladies and gentlemen, for this very cordial reception, and beg leave to express my gratitude to the gentlemen who, by their invitation, have afforded me an opportunity to contribute, however humbly, towards the completion of a work which, for more than a quarter of a century, I have regarded as of prime importance to the country, and of special value to my native city and State, and for the promotion of which, during that period, I have labored as opportunity offered. I do not expect the statement of facts I shall make to be accepted without many grains of allowance by those of my hearers who have not visited the trans-Missouri portion of our country; and shall not be surprised if many of you leave the hall with the opinion that I have dealt largely in exaggeration. Yet it is my purpose to speak within the limits of truth, and to make no statement that is not justified by my personal observation, or authorities that all are bound to recognize, or the concurrent statements of numbers of inhabitants of, and travellers through, the country of which I am to speak.

The truth is, that however well informed a man may be and however large the grasp of his mind, if his life has been passed between the Atlantic and the Mississippi river, he cannot fully conceive the strange contrasts between the characteristics of the Atlantic and Pacific portions of our country. The difference in topography is marked, and recognized by all; but as to the subtle differences of climate, soil, temperature and atmosphere, experience, alone, can impart conviction.

About two years ago, it was my privilege, in connection with my colleagues on the Committee of Ways Means of the National House of Representatives, to traverse the entire route of the Union and Central Pacific Road by daylight, and to visit Salt Lake City, which was, as all know, located in the heart of the "Great Desert," that it might be the centre of a Mormon empire that would be guarded by the forces of Nature against Gentile intrusion. After having somewhat studied California, with San Francisco as our head-quarters, we passed up the coast to the mouth of the Columbia river, along that beautiful stream to its confluence with the Willamette, and up the Willamette to Portland, Oregon, as a new point of departure for observation, visiting thence on one line of steamers, Oregon city, with its immense flouring and woolen mills, and on another, the grandeur (for beauty does not express it) of the Columbia river beyond the Cascades and onward to the Dalles. Though that region had so long been a matter of interest to me, the study of which had afforded so much pleasure, each day revealed new and strange conditions, and imbued me with a fresh sense, not only of the extent of our country, but of the grandeur and infinite variety of its resources and the beneficence and power of the Almighty, in adapting all parts of it to the sustenance and comfort of man. But of this hereafter.

Let me first invite your attention to facts within the memory of some of my auditors, which show that the resources of the new northwest and its adaptability to railroad purposes are not, as is sometimes intimated, of recent discovery, but have long been known, and that the route of the Northern Pacific Railroad is that originally proposed, because it is the shortest and best by which to connect the seaboard at Baltimore, Philadelphia, New York, Boston and Portland, Me., with the waters of Puget Sound and the commerce of the ancient East, which is now the West, the march towards which, of American ideas is illustrating again the truth that,

"Westward the course of empire takes its way."

## *Pacific Railroad History.*

During the summer of 1845, twenty-six years ago, Asa Whitney, of New York, who had spent many years in China, and sought, by all such agencies as were at the command of private enterprise, information about the country lying between Lake Michigan and Puget Sound, did me the honor to seek my acquaintance and bring to my attention the subject of a railroad from the base of the Lake to some point in Oregon, on the waters of Puget Sound or the Columbia river, or to a point on each. The whole subject was new to me; but Mr. Whitney came prepared to enlighten those who were ignorant, and to inspire with faith those who doubted. His general views were in print, and embodied columns of statistics, obtained from official sources, and many facts reported by persons who had travelled more or less through the region which the proposed road was to traverse. The magnitude of the subject inspired me, and my enthusiasm for his great project induced Mr. Whitney, despite the disparity in our years, to favor me with frequent conferences, and to bring to my attention whatever information relating to the subject he obtained. Early in the year 1846, I felt justified, by the growth of sentiment in its favor, in undertaking to secure him an opportunity to present his project to a public meeting of the citizens of Philadelphia. To induce a sufficient number of gentlemen to act as officers of the meeting was the work of time. I found few who took an interest in, or believed in the feasibility of, the project. Some said that a railroad so far north would not be available for as many months in the year as the Pennsylvania canals were; that it would be buried in snow more than half the year. Others cried, "What madness to talk of a railroad more than two thousand miles long through that wilderness, when it is impossible to build one over the Alleghanies!" [Laughter and applause.]

As I went from man to man with Mr. Whitney's invaluable collection of facts and figures, I discovered that the doubts with which the work must contend were infinite in number, and it was not until six months had elapsed that a sufficient number of well-known citizens to constitute the officers of a meeting had consented to sign the call for one and act as such. But patience and perseverence accomplish a good deal in this world. The cause had gained adherents, and, as I find by reference to the papers of that day, the meeting for which I had so long labored was held in the Chinese Museum, on the evening of December 23d, 1846. Some of these, my venerable friends who sit around me, probably remember the occasion, as I see among them some who acted as officers. His Honor, John Swift, then Mayor of the city, presided. Col. James Page, Hons. Richard Vaux, William M. Meredith and John F. Belsterling, with Mr. David S. Brown and Mr. Charles B. Trego (all of whom still survive) were among the vice presidents; and Senator Wm. A. Crabb, now deceased, and William D. Kelley served as secretaries. The speakers were

Messrs. Whitney, Josiah Randall, Peter A. Browne and William D. Kelley.

Mayor Swift, with a few cautious words commendatory of his great enterprise, introduced Mr. Whitney, who stated, with great clearness, his project, and the advantages that would result from its execution. It was, he said, to be a railroad from Lake Michigan to a point on navigable water in Oregon. He believed that it could be constructed on a line about 2400 miles in length; and that he and his associates hoped to be able to build it in twenty years, if the Government would grant sixty miles breadth of land for the whole distance. When asked how he would make land in that remote northern wilderness available for the building of a road, he described the character of the climate, and showed that north of the forty-ninth degree of north latitude, and in valleys extending up to the fifty-sixth degree, the climate was in summer as genial as that of Southern Pennsylvania; and asserted emphatically that a railroad through that section would be less obstructed by snow than one through Central New York or Pennsylvania.

His scheme was to organize a vast system of immigration from the cities of the Eastern States and from Europe; the workmen were to be paid in part in land, and a corps was to be detailed to prepare a part of each farm for cultivation the next year, so that when the laborers of the second year should go forward they would leave behind them those of the first as farmers and guardsmen of the road; by this process many millions of poor and oppressed people would be lifted to the dignity of free-holding American citizens, and the great route for the commerce of the world would be established amid the development of the boundless resources of the yet new Northwest. (Applause.)

At the close of an eloquent address, the late Josiah Randall, Esq., submitted a series of resolutions, from which I quote the following, which were heartily adopted:

"Whereas, the completion of a railroad from Lake Michigan to the Pacific would secure the carrying of the greater portion of the commerce of the world to American enterprise, and open to it the markets of Japan and the vast empire of China, of all India, and of all the islands of the Pacific and Indian Oceans, together with those of the Western Coast of Mexico and South America;

And, whereas, we have in our public lands a fund sufficient for and appropriate to the construction of so great and beneficent a work; and the proposition of Asa Whitney, Esq., of New York, to construct a railroad from Lake Michigan to the Pacific for the grant of a strip of land 60 miles wide, offers a feasible and cheap, if not the only plan for the early completion of an avenue from ocean to ocean; therefore,

"*Resolved*, That we cordially approve of the project of Asa Whitney, Esq., for the construction of a railroad to the Pacific, and respectfully petition Congress to grant or set apart, before the close of the present session, the lands prayed for by Mr. Whitney for this purpose."

It was also resolved to send copies of the resolutions and proceedings of the meeting to our senators and members of Congress, and to the Governor of the Commonwealth, with the request that he would bring the subject to the attention of the Legislature.

Encouraged by this success, Mr. Whitney visited other cities, and brought his plans before the people. On the 4th of January, 1847, he addressed an immense meeting in the Tabernacle, New York, which was presided over by the mayor and participated in by the leading men of that city. His remarks were listened to, but at their close a mob took possession of the hall and denounced the project as a swindle, declaring thas it was an attempt on the part of a band of conspirators to defraud the people by inducing the Government to make an immense grant of land for an impracticable project.

This was the initial movement of a powerful and organized opposition, before which Mr. Whitney retired, silenced in his effort to promote one of the grandest works ever conceived by an American citizen. (Applause.) But his labors had not been in vain. On the 23d of June, 1848, Hon. James Pollock, the present Director of the United States Mint, who does me the honor to listen to me, and who was then in Congress from this State, as

chairman of a special committee appointed in accordance with a resolution he had offered, presented a favorable report on the project of a Pacific Railroad, recommending that steps be taken to secure adequate explorations and surveys of the trans-Mississippi country. The "madness" of the project was still laughed at even by "grave and reverened" senators; and it was not until the 3d of March, 1853, that the President signed an act authorizing the Secretary of War, under his direction, "to employ such portion of the corps of topographical engineers and such other persons as he may deem necessary to make such explorations and surveys as he may deem advisable, to ascertain the most practicable and economical route for a railroad from the Mississippi river to the Pacific ocean." Effect was given to this resolution at the earliest day, but it was not until the 27th of February, 1855, that the Secretary of War was able to submit to the President, for communication to Congress, the reports of the several surveying parties. The first of these reports were given to the public by order of Congress in the latter part of that year. They fill thirteen large quarto volumes, and I shall have occasion to refer to them hereafter.

*The Pennsylvania Central Road.*

As experience is a trusted teacher it may be well to pause and examine the condition of the railroad interests of the country at that time. At the close of 1846, we had 4930 miles of road in operation, 297 of which had been completed during that year. A system of continuous railroad had not been proposed. Until about that time the function of railroads had been assumed to be to connect water-courses. Thus the Columbia Railroad constructed by our State authorities, connected the waters of the Pennsylvania canals with those of the Delaware river; the Camden and Amboy road connected the waters of the Delaware with those of the Raritan; from Philadelphia to Baltimore, until 1838, communication was by steamboat from Philadelphia to Newcastle, thence by rail to Frenchtown, thence by steamboat to Baltimore. The route from Boston to New York was by railroad from Boston to Providence, and by steamboat thence to New York. These connecting links of road soon developed a commerce, not equal to their capacity but beyond that of available water conveyance, and thus demonstrated the necessity of a more general resort to roads. Hence the subject of the expansion of our system was attracting attention. The construction of the Pennsylvania Central road was under consideration. On the 3d of April, 1846, the Legislature, after much and violent controversy, had consented to give the madcaps, who were willing to engage in such a project, a charter; but to prevent them from practising fraud, by peddling the franchise or holding it for sinister purposes, the act required that $2,500,000 of stock should be subscribed, and that the enormous sum of $250,000 should be paid in before the issuing of letters patent. Most of you, doubtless, suppose that the requisite subscription was obtained at once. No; nearly twelve months were required to induce the enterprising men of Philadelphia to risk two millions and a half of dollars in building a road over the Alleghanies. "The grades on the road," it was said, "would be impracticable; the heavy snows and long winter would render the road unavailable; the project was a mad one." Those only who remember the efforts required to induce the people of Pennsylvania to make that small subscription would believe the story, could it be faithfully told. The active young men of this day would regard it as a pungent satire.

Town meetings were held, and "block-committees" were appointed, by whom citizens were solicited to subscribe for five shares or three or one, for the sake of

the experiment, even though the investment might be unproductive. Meetings of draymen and porters were held, and they were shown that if each would take a share, it would help the enterprize; that if the road should prove a success they would get good interest on their money with great increase of business; and if not, it would have been wisely spent in promoting an enterprise which, in the judgment of many good men, promised great benefit to the City and State.

I have spoken of the business men of Philadelphia, but the appeal was not to them alone; it was to the people of Pennsylvania. This was to be a Pennsylvania road, and by the act of incorporation the commissioners for receiving subscriptions were required to open books at Pittsburg, Hollidaysburg, Harrisburg, and all the chief towns along the line of the road, as well as in Philadelphia; and the energy, enterprise, and capital of the whole State stood appalled at the magnitude and doubtful character of an undertaking to build a continuous line of railroad from Philadelphia to Pittsburg.

It was not until the 30th of March, 1847, but three days less than one year from the granting of the charter that the petty subscription required was obtained, letters patent issued, and a board of directors organized. And it remained for some time thereafter a grave question whether capital could be obtained by subscription or loan to complete the road.

But by the middle of October, 1850, a single track was completed from Harrisburg, its then point of departure, to Hollidaysburg, at the foot of the Alleghany mountains. The triumph was immense; and on the 18th of October, 1850, the event was celebrated by an excursion, which was enjoyed by many prominent business men and other friends of the road. In the evening a meeting was held over a pleasant dinner, at which I remember my friend, General Patterson (pointing to the general, who sat on the stage in company with Governor Geary), and his friend, old General Riley, were speakers. The late President Buchanan and Joseph R. Ingersoll, Esq., also deceased, spoke. At the close of a very brilliant speech, my friend, Morton McMichael, Esq., did me the honor to introduce me as one who had been an early and efficient friend of the road.

From a musty copy of the *North American* now before me, I find that, among other things, I expressed my pride "in the fact that I was a Philadelphian, a member of that community which, with aid from but a single township—that of Allegheny—had, in the face of a host of discouragements, embarked their capital, enterprise, energy and skill in the construction of the magnificent road over which we had travelled that day, and which, though not yet completed, was sufficiently advanced to earn in a few years, the means for its completion, should they not be supplied from other sources." And, alluding to what was then my favorite project, I said:

"The English mail for Calcutta will yet travel over our Pennsylvania Railroad, and its iron ribs will groan under the weight of commodities passing to and fro between the 250,000,000 of people east of the Atlantic and the 750,000,000 west of the Pacific. The discovery of our Continent by Columbus was accidental; but the builders of this road and its several continuations through the Western States are vindicating his sagacity. He sailed due west from Europe to find a shorter route to the wealth of India. He was right; the fact that he encountered a continent did not increase the distance between the points; it did but demonstrate the necessity for a new mode of conveyance. This the railroad and locomotive supply. The passage of the two oceans by steam and the crossing of our country on a railroad will reduce the time requisite for a voyage from London to Canton to less than thirty days.

"Columbus was no enthusiast. He looked calmly and gravely at facts, and spoke the words of sober wisdom; and so, let folly sneer as it may, do those who speak of the Pennsylvania road as a link in a chain of commercial facilities which is to girdle the earth." [Applause.]

And again:

"The Mississippi Valley is not our Western country, nor is the Pacific coast of our country the 'far West' we look to. Columbus would go west to the Indies; and we will do it. The riches of our West, now the world's East, will lade our road, stimulate our agriculture, develop our vast mineral resources, quicken and expand our enterprise, and drop their fatness throughout our borders." [Applause.]

I find that, when somewhat laughed at for this outburst of subdued enthusiasm, I replied by saying:

"Why, you can find in Philadelphia to-day more men clamorous for a road from St. Louis to San Francisco than you could who believed in the possibility of constructing a continuous road over the mountains hence to Pittsburg six years ago."

This, you will remember, was after the acquisition of California and the discovery of her gold-fields.

### *A Quarter of a Century.*

But to return to 1846, a quarter of a century ago. Let no man think that the Pacific Railroad then projected was to run to San Francisco, or elsewhere than to the heart of the unorganized Territory of Oregon, which extended from the 42d to the 49th parallel of latitude, and embraced what is now the State of Oregon and Washington Territory, into which no settlers had yet gone.

There was then no San Francisco. Not a cabin or hut stood within the now corporate limits of that beautiful and prosperous city. California, Nevada, Arizona and New Mexico, were still Mexican territory. Neither science nor observation had detected the deposits of gold and silver, or the agricultural capabilities of that vast region of country. The great railroad centre of the West, Chicago, had not yet come into public view. The less than 10,000 people who had gathered at the confluence of the Chicago river with Lake Michigan had no presentiment that the swamp in which they dwelt would, in less than twenty years, be filled up and raised nearly twenty feet, to provide drainage for the streets of the most enterprising and remarkable city in the world, of its age. Michigan then had a population of less than 250,000, and Wisconsin and Iowa each but 100,000; and civilization had not yet penetrated the wide region then known as Minnesota territory, where the census takers, four years later, found but 6,038 people. Four years later there were but 91,635 people in California, which had then been ceded to us by Mexico, and admitted to the Union as a State, and whose recently discovered deposits of gold had attracted immigrants from every clime. There was no government in Kansas and Nebraska, that whole fertile region being in possession of the Indian and the buffalo. The name of that busy centre of river and railroad commerce, Omaha, had not been heard by English-speaking people, and the vast mineral, grazing and agricultural region through which the Union and Central Pacific railroad is now doing a profitable and rapidly increasing business, was noted by geographers as the "Great American Desert." Philadelphia had no railroad connection with Pittsburg, Pittsburg none with Cincinnati or Chicago, nor any of these with St. Louis. The northwestern part of our State was known as the "wild-cat country," in which it was regarded as a misfortune to own land unless it was timbered and on the banks of a mountain stream; and properties in that wide section in which coal and petroleum have since been discovered were sold every few years for taxes, because people could not afford to own land in such a cold, mountainous, unproductive and inaccessible country. [Laughter and applause.]

Surely the world moves and time does work wonders. What railroads we have you know; what railroads we are to have you only begin to suspect. In Europe, during this quarter of a century, dynasties and the boundaries of empires have changed, but the increase of population has been scarcely perceptible. The oppressions of the feudal past linger there, and cannot be shaken off. But here, where man is free, and nature offers boundless returns to enterprise, broad empires have risen, embracing towns, cities, and states; and millions of people born in many lands with poverty and oppression as their only birthright, are now, as American citizens, enjoying all the comforts and refinements of civilization, and with capital rivaling that of European princes, originating and pressing forward great enterprises which are in the next quarter of a century to work more marvellous changes than any I have alluded to. Yes, ladies and gentlemen, were supernal power to unfold to our view our country as it shall be a quarter of a century hence, the most far-seeing and sanguine of us would regard the reality as a magnificent delusion. Our extension of territory and law, great as it has been, is of small consequence in comparison with the achievements of mind in the empire of science and art, whereby man is enabled to produce ten-fold, and in many departments of productive industry, a hundred-fold as much as he could twenty-five years ago by the same amount of labor. New roads are to be built; new towns, cities and states to be created; new resources developed; and the sluggish people of the Orient are to be awakened to their own interests and induced to contribute their vast share to the progress and commerce of the world. The vision that filled the soul of Columbus was a grand one; but that which opens to our view, and should possess and animate us, is as much grander and more beneficent as the civilization and arts of the close of the 19th are superior to those of the dawning days of the 14th century.

## *The Northern Pacific Railroad.*

I regard the construction of the Northern Pacific Railroad as chief among the great works of the future, and believe that while it will be a magnificent monument to its builders and promoters, and abundantly reward their enterprise and labor, its construction will add inconceivably to the wealth, power and influence of the nation. It will open to settlement under the homestead and pre-emption laws a territory that would accommodate all the peasantry of Europe, and, by the development of its boundless and varied mineral and agricultural resources, lift millions of men from poverty to wealth, and enable many who are burdens upon society to bless it by their prosperity. [Applause.]

These are well considered convictions. If I am mistaken, I have, as I have shown you, cherished the delusion through the greater part of my manhood; and the study of many authorities, much intercourse with men, and extended travel have only served to confirm it. Nor do I now express them for the first time. On the 26th of April, 1866, a bill proposing to authorize the government to aid in the construction of the Northern Pacific Railroad was under consideration by Congress, and I participated in the discussion. By reference to the *Globe*, I find, that after having characterized the construction of the road as a matter of not only National, but world-wide importance, I said:

"From Lake Superior to Puget Sound! A railroad stretching from Lake Superior to Puget Sound, a distance of 1800 miles! To open to civilization an empire longer and broader than Western Europe, from the southern vinelands of sunny Spain on the one hand to the hyperborean forests of Norway on the other! Yes, sir; an empire equal in extent to England, Ireland, Scotland, France, Belgium, the German States, Austria, Holland, Italy, Switzerland, Denmark, Sweden, Norway, Spain and Portugal.

"We fail, Mr. Speaker, to understand our relations to the age in which we live and our duties to mankind, because we fail to appreciate the grand dimensions and unimagined resources of our country. We would regard ourselves as giants did we estimate ourselves in proportion to possessions so grand in a country so abounding in multiform resources, so undeveloped, and so sparsely settled.

"The region through which it is proposed to construct this road, exceeding in extent all the countries I have named, also embodies more mineral wealth than they all combined ever possessed. But what is its condition? It is a wilderness. Almost every acre of it is still innocent of the tread of a tax collector. It yields the Government no revenue. Along the Pacific coast a few thriving villages dot it. Some of them will one day be great cities, but they are now on the borders of a vast wilderness."

## *Compared with Other Routes.*

But there are those who, while admitting the vast extent and wonderful resources of the country, assert that it is unfit for occupancy by communities by reason of its high latitude and the altitude of its mountains. They present all the objections that were made to the construction of the Pennsylvania Railroad. "The mountains are too high," "the snows are too deep, and lie too long!" Are not these objections as groundless in this case as they were in that? Let us see. Government surveys and other observations show, beyond reasonable question, that a railroad between the 46th and 49th parallels will have a better route than any other road north of the 32d degree, which line has the drawback of a summer climate that is so nearly tropical as to interfere with travel and the general transit of goods. I am convinced that the country through which the Northern Pacific Railroad is to pass will, twenty-five years hence, contain double the population that will then be found along the line of the road which connects Omaha and Sacramento. Indeed I believe I would be within the bounds of reasonable prediction if I made my proposition embrace the continuation of the road from the City of Sacramento to San Francisco, notwithstanding the wondrous attractions California presents to those who are seeking a new home and more profitable field for enterprise.

The Central route must create its way traffic; none awaited its construction. From Omaha to Sacramento not a navigable stream crosses the route of the Union and Central road; nor does one approach it. Let me not be understood as disparaging the value of this road, or as intimating that it is not already doing a profitable business, or that it will not, as every other railroad in this country has done, create a constantly increasing volume of business that will enable it to rapidly decrease its rates for freight and travel, while increasing its income and net profits. Indeed it is already doing this, and its present charges for freight and travel compare very favorably with those of 1869.

Yes, it has its way business to create, and is doing it rapidly. Witness the two branch roads already constructed, one from Denver to Cheyenne, and the other from Salt Lake City to Ogden. Before the main line was built, who dreamed of railroads along either of those valleys? Behold, also, the enormous development of the coal and iron fields at Evanston, a little west of Cheyenne, and more than 500 miles west of Omaha. Two years ago the fact was proudly announced that both coal and iron had been discovered at Evanston; and now the place is marked by the smoke and din of forges, furnaces, rolling-mills, machine shops, and preparations are making for the manufacture of Bessemer steel rails, the construction of the works having been commenced. [Applause.]

Look, too, at the marvellous development by "gentile" hands of the silver mines in southern Utah, to which the Mormons, Brigham Young having driven the first spike about a fortnight ago, are extending their branch road in order to carry silver ore, the transportation of which from the mines to Swansea, England, taxes it $40 a ton. This tax will be saved when some American shall be enterprising enough to put up smelting works in a country in which coal and rich ores abound. Yes, British vessels coming to New York and Philadelphia with salt or iron return freighted with the ores of southern Utah, because we have not the enterprise to smelt it.

Look, again, at the development of the wool trade. In many of the valleys along the line of the Central and Union road there are flocks numbering not thirty, not fifty, not a hundred sheep, as in the old States, but thousands; and some flocks numbering more than ten thousand head now range valleys in the very heart of the

"Great American Desert," where it was supposed civilization would never find an abode.

What a field for genius, enterprise and industry! It will, at no distant day, swarm with men of grit. There are thousands of young men in this city filling small offices, or in some other way picking up a precarious living, getting through the world somehow, never knowing whether both ends will meet at the end of any month, who, were they to go to this country, carrying with them the knowledge gained in our furnaces, machine shops or factories, would in a few years find themselves at the head of large establishments and commanding hundreds of employees. [Applause.] I rejoice in the fact that the Grand Army of the Republic is organizing one-armed and one-legged soldiers to go and settle in colonies upon the public lands, on the theory that their wives and children will share their labors in securing a homestead and honest independence. The scheme is as judicious as it is noble, and the poor disabled fellows will, I doubt not, in a few years write back to their less energetic but unmutilated comrades to come and work for and be fed and clothed by them. [Laughter and applause.]

These branch roads and expanding industries are but some of the many precursors and sure pledges of the immense sources of traffic that are to rise along a road, the drinking water for many of whose agents, as well as for the supply of many of its engines, is brought in tanks over alkaline plains for hundreds of miles, and one of the summits of which, at Sherman, is a mile and a-half above the topmost spire of Philadelphia, and 3285 feet higher than the most elevated summit on the Northern road,—that at Deer Lodge Pass.

*Growth of Railroad Traffic.*

That this road will create business for itself, and speedily return the capital embarked in its construction I am abundantly persuaded. This opinion is confirmed by the highest authority on such questions known to railroad men in this country, H. V. Poor, Esq., who, in his admirable sketch of the railroads of the United States, published last year, says:

"It is safe to estimate that the railroad tonnage of the country would duplicate itself as often as once in ten years, were there no increase of line or population, from the progress made in its industries and in the mechanic arts."

Mr. Poor amply sustains this proposition by facts deduced from the railroad history of the country, and says:

"Our means will increase just in the degree in which we render available the wealth that now lies dormant in our soil."

Speaking of the year 1869, he says:

"The tonnage traffic of the railroads constructed the past year, at only one thousand tons to the mile, will equal five million tons, having a value of $750,000,000! Every road constructed adds five times its value to the aggregate value of the property of the country. The cost of the works constructed the past year will equal at least $150,000,000. The increased value, consequently, of property due to the construction will equal $600,000,000."

These observations of Mr. Poor are specially applicable to the Northern Pacific Road, the construction of which will not only create an immense volume of through travel, but develop a region not exceeded in native wealth by any equal area on the face of the globe; which abounds in the precious and other metals, in wheat-lands and lumber forests, and embraces the natural home of the sheep and goat, and grazing fields in which herds of cattle large enough to supply our entire market, may graze throughout the year, growing and fattening upon natural grasses, which in the dry atmosphere of the country, do not decompose as ours do when exposed to the weather, but cure where they grow, and feed herds of buffalo, elk, antelope and mountain sheep the year round.

*The New Northwest.*

Minnesota, through which the road will be completed by October, from Lake Superior to the Red river, 266 miles, is the great wheat field of our country. It is a land of lakes and rivers, of forest and prairie. Its farmers are prosperous and contented. Its population numbered 6077 in 1850; had swollen to 172,022 by 1860; and was found to be 436,057 in 1870. The value of its farm products as reported by the census of 1870 was $33,350,923; the cash value of its farms $97,621,691; and its production of wheat during 1869 was about 19,000,000 bushels. It contains (listen, young men who are working for wages,) 53,459,840 acres, of which but 3,637,671 are occupied. The remaining 50,000,000 await your coming for their development. [Applause.] It is not yet fourteen years since the lumbermen of Minnesota were fed on wheat imported from other States. Yet the wheat crop raised during 1870, from the small part of the State then occupied, is believed to have been not less than 30,000,000 bushels. Time will not permit me even to indicate the immense resources of this State in lumber, iron, slate, and other commodities, that bear transportation; and I leave Minnesota with the remark that when the winter traveler westward on the Northern Pacific Railroad, shall leave her limits and cross the Red river of the North, he will leave behind him the coldest part of the road and that most liable to obstruction by snow. The only other point at which he will, even under exceptional circumstances, meet with as great a depression of the mercury will be in the neighborhood of Fort Stevenson, in Central Dakota.

### *A Genial Climate.*

How, ladies and gentlemen, shall I help you to understand something about the climate of the country west of Minnesota? To us of the East it seems incredible that the temperature of the mountains, along a line running between the 47th and 49th parallels should be so mild; yet so it is; and the climate of Washington Territory, along the 49th parallel, is more equable the year round, and milder in winter than that of Philadelphia or Baltimore. Indeed, the mean temperature at Olympia, at the head of Puget Sound, is that of Norfolk, Va., but the dwellers on the Sound are strangers alike to the extreme heat of a Virginia summer and the extreme cold of its winter. There cattle are not housed at any season, and thrive upon the grasses they find on the plains. In the western valleys of Washington Territory, winter is unknown. Snow comes occasionally to remind settlers of what they used to see in the States of the East; but it never lies. But once since 1847, when the first settlements were made, have cattle been deprived by snow for three consecutive days, of the natural pasture furnished throughout the winter months west of the mountains in Washington Territory and Oregon.

The winter climate upon the mountains of Idaho, Montana and Dakota is more severe; but in their valleys the buffalo, elk and antelope have been accustomed to winter; and domestic cattle, worn by labor in the service of exploring expeditions and transportation companies, are turned into the valleys and herded, and come out in the spring fat and ready for another tour of duty. This is so inconsistent with our experience, that I beg leave to fortify the statement with a single authority, the equal to which I could produce by scores. I will, however, content myself with a brief extract from the report of explorations of the Yellowstone, made by Gen. Reynolds, of the Engineer Corps of the U. S. Army, who wintered, in 1860, in the valley of Deer Creek, in which the Northern Pacific Road will attain its greatest elevation and cross the Rocky Mountains On this subject he says:

"Throughout the whole of the season's march, the subsistence of our animals had been obtained by grazing after we had reached camp in the afternoon, and for an hour or two between the dawn of day and our time of starting. The consequence was that when we reached our winter quarters there were but few animals in the train that were in a condition to have continued the march without a generous grain diet. Poorer and more broken down creatures it would be difficult to find. In the spring all were in as fine condition for commencing another season's work as could be desired. A greater change in their appearance could not have been produced, even if they had been grain-fed and stable-housed all winter. *Only one was lost*, the furious storm of December coming on before it had gained sufficient strength to endure it. *This fact, that seventy exhausted animals turned out to winter on the plains on the first of November, came out in the best condition, and with the loss of but one, is the most forcible commentary I can make on the quality of the grass and the character of the winter.*"

This seems incredible, but many degrees to the north of our territories are immense valleys, which, if the testimony of British officers, civil and military, of missionaries and settlers who have dwelt there for years, may be believed, rival Minnesota in wheat-producing capacity, and eastern Oregon and Washington Territory in the mildness of their mean temperature. Exploration and settlement have abolished "The Great American Desert," of which these territories formed a conspicuous part, and it no longer finds a place on maps. And the Mormons have demonstrated that by conducting the melting snow of the mountains to the foot-hills and valleys, the whole region can be made to bloom as the rose, and bear crops of cereals, roots and fruit equal to those yielded by the best farms in the choice valleys of Pennsylvania.

### *Wool and Beet-Root Sugar.*

Since these apparently inhospitable regions have been penetrated by railroads, and mining adventure has created settlements up even to the northern boundary of Dakota, Montana and Idaho, we are discovering why we have not succeeded in raising wool, and why we are still, while boasting of our agricultural productions, dependent upon non-manufacturing countries which are not famed for their agricultural resources or skill, for our supply of wool. The reason is found in the fact that we have not carried flocks to those portions of our country which are pre-eminently adapted to the support of wool-bearing animals.

Mountainous and volcanic as are our territories, which extend from the 32d to the 49th parallel, they are peculiarly adapted to sheep culture. With their settlement we shall become the greatest wool-producing country of the world, though our present production gives but small promise of such a result. The sources and amount of the wool-clip of 1868 were in round figures about as follows:

| | POUNDS. |
|---|---|
| British North American Provinces, | 10,000,000 |
| Australia, South America, and Africa, | 76,000,000 |
| United States, | 100,000,000 |
| Spain, Portugal and Italy, | 119,000,000 |
| France, | 123,000,000 |
| European Russia, | 125,000,000 |
| Germany, | 200,000,000 |
| Great Britain, | 260,000,000 |
| Asia, | 470,000,000 |

Thus it appears that Asia, Australia, Africa and South America, which furnish no such markets for mutton as the commercial and manufacturing centres of Europe and this country, and where sheep must be raised for the wool alone, are its great producers. Why is wool chief among the staple exports of South America? Because her pampas present the same conditions as our territories. Why has Australia built up a great city more by its wool trade than its gold? It is because her sheep walks are dry and covered with bunch grass, which cures itself in the field as is the case in our territories. Why does Asia produce more wool than Great Britain and Germany together, and almost as much as Great Britain, Germany and the United States? It is because the grasses of the elevated plains on which her countless flocks of sheep and goats range are the same nutritious, aromatic grasses upon which the elk, the buffalo and the mountain sheep have fed through all time upon "The Great American Desert" of America. [Applause.]

Under the impulse given to this interest by the Union and Central road, flocks numbering thousands, collected in Illinois, Wisconsin, Iowa, and more eastern States have been transferred to such plains and valleys as are accessible by the road, and where the expense of raising sheep is but the cost of the first flock and of herding. There the finest wool may be produced, and with increasing railroad facilities, mining, manufacturing, and commercial centers will furnish markets for mutton, and add to the wool grower's profits. To say that the wool-clip of the United States, as shown by the census of 1880, will exceed that of Great Britain is not to offer a prediction, but to assert a foregone conclusion; and it is also safe to say that the clip of that year will embrace not only wool of all grades of sheep, but of the Cashmere, Angora and other goats, the value of whose hair is so well known to manufacturers and merchants. But more than this, remembering the rapidity with which flocks increase, I predict that at an early day our wool clip will equal that of Asia,* which will insure us supremacy in the manufacture of the entire range of woolen and worsted goods.

And with this increased production of wool, will come another great industry. You will question my judgment when I tell you that the territory along the 46th, 47th, 48th and 49th degrees of latitude high up the mountain sides is to be a great sugar-producing country. Yet as sure as that the world moves and science helps man to supply his wants cheaply, the country along the routes of the Union and Central and the Northern Pacific Railroads will in a few years produce immense quantities of sugar. Of course, I speak of beet-root sugar, the manufacture of which will thrive not only along our northern boundary, but in the more northern settlements of the Assineboine and Saskatchewan valleys as it does in Russia, Sweden and Norway; as it is already doing in California, Illinois and Wisconsin, and will do in all of the States of the Northwest. Many causes conspire to make the introduction of this industry into our country a necessity; and in the region of cheap land, abundant fuel and pure water from the mountain snows, in which the cost of transportation more than doubles the price of cane sugar, it must find an early and extensive development.

To show that these views are not new or strained, permit me to bring to your

* On the day after the delivery of the text, my attention was invited to the following striking confirmation of my views furnished by M. Alcan, Professor of Spinning and Weaving at the Conservatoire Impérial des Arts, &c.

APPROXIMATE PRODUCTION OF WOOLS IN 1866.

[Translated from Alcan's "Etudes sur les Arts Textile à l'Exposition Universalle de 1867" for the April number of the Bulletin of the National Association of Wool Manufacturers.]

"The quantity of the production of wools in weight may be reckoned approximately by the number of sheep in each country. We estimate the sheep at the numbers indicated in the following table:

| | NO. OF SHEEP. |
|---|---|
| France, | 30,000,000 |
| Algeria, | 10,000,000 |
| Russia, | 54,000,000 |
| England, | 26,376,000 |
| Austria, | 27,000,090 |
| Prussia, Zollverein, | 24,000,000 |
| Ottoman Empire, | 32,000,000 |
| Australia, | 35,000,000 |
| Cape of Good Hope, | 12,000,000 |
| New Zealand, | 15,000,000 |
| The Equator or la Plata, | 30,000,000 |
| Spain, | 20,000,090 |
| Italy, | 8,500,000 |
| Belgium, | 3,000,000 |
| The Low Countries, | 1,500,000 |
| Portugal, | 2,417,000 |
| Total, | 330,783,000 |

"*Remarks upon the numbers of the preceding table.*—If we compare the present number of sheep as indicated in the preceding table with the numbers heretofore given by us, it will not be difficult to recognize that while the production of sheep has decreased or remained stationary in Europe, it has prodigiously developed itself in the new countries beyond the ocean. Thus, for example, the number of wool-bearing animals has diminished in England, in Spain, and even in France, if we do not include Algeria; and it has remained nearly stationary in the different parts of Germany. On the contrary, the development exhibits an enormous progression at the Cape, in Australia, and, above all, in La Plata. In seven years, from 1860 to 1867, the production has been raised nearly 108 per cent. for the first of these countries, nearly 100 per cent. for the second, and 268 per cent. for the third.

notice a letter I had the honor to address to Dr. Latham, a cultivated and intelligent gentleman, who, after spending years in the Territories, devoted last winter to bringing their resources to the attention of the wool-growers and woolen manufacturers of the Eastern States;

"HOUSE OF REPRESENTATIVES,
*Washington, D. C., Dec.* 18, 1870.

"DR. H. LATHAM,
"LARAMIE,
*Wyoming Territory.*

"DEAR SIR.—I must admit that I thought some of the statements you made when I met you at Laramie, and you were kind enough to accompany us eastward were exaggerated; but subsequent observation and study have satisfied me that you did not fully indicate the capacity of the territories for varied production and the sustenance of a numerous and prosperous population.

"Two industries, each of primary importance to the country, should be introduced at an early day because both will find there, the conditions under which they may be brought almost immediately to absolute perfection. I mean the growth of wool, both from the Angora and Cashmere goats and sheep, and the production of beet-root sugar. For the latter, Grant in his admirable little book, says the primary essentials are cheap land and fuel and pure water. All these you have wherever the melting snow of the mountains can be carried for irrigation, and in the neighborhood of all your mountain streams. Your natural grasses and aromatic herbage are identical with those of the great sheep-fields of Asia and Australia; and should you establish the production of the beet, and the manufacture of sugar on a large scale, you will find, as it has been found everywhere else, that three tons of the refuse beet, from which the saccharine matter has been expressed, will be equivalent to two tons of the best hay in sustaining and fattening sheep and cattle. It, therefore, seems to me that you will render a very important service, not only to your own section, but to the country at large, if, by making known these peculiar resources you promote the establishment of two such vital industries. Either of them will doubtless succeed if undertaken by proper hands; but both should be established, as each will contribute to the success of the other.

"Again thanking you for the important information you have given me, and wishing you abundant success in your efforts to promote the development of this extended and interesting portion of our country, I remain

"Yours, very truly,
"WM. D. KELLEY.

## *Montana—Lieut. Doane's Report.*

Thanks to the admirable scientific training given our army officers at West Point, and the desire of that distinguished soldier and son of Pennsylvania, Gen. Winfield S. Hancock, [applause,] to ascertain and disclose the resources of the district of which he is in command, we have a recent official report on the characteristics of a hitherto unexplored section of Montana, the wonders of which not only exceed those of Niagara and the geysers of California, but rival in magnitude and extraordinary combination those of the Yo Semite, the canons of Colorado and the geysers of Iceland. But I cannot pause even to allude to these. Tourists and men of science will give the world many a description of them. My purpose is to illustrate the climate and the fertility not only of the valleys but of the mountains, which bear trees rising beyond one hundred feet in height at an elevation which in New York or New England would mark the region of perpetual snow.

I have here Executive Document No. 51, of the Third Session, Forty-first Congress. It is the report (and you will see that it is quite brief) of Lieut. Gustavus C. Doane, upon the so-called Yellowstone expedition of 1870. It is Lieut Doane's account of a brief tour made by the Surveyor General of Montana, whose duty it was to survey the yet hidden region of his district, and who applied to Gen. Hancock for an escort to enable him to do so with safety. The General promptly complied with the request, and put the escort under the charge of Lieut. Doane, with instructions to keep a record, noting the condition of the barometer and thermometer, and the elevation of each day's camp, and to report these and such other facts as might in his opinion be of general interest.

The party were out thirty-four days. Their point of departure was Fort Ellis, which is at an elevation of 4911 feet, and at which the thermometer at noon, on the day of their departure, August 22, 1870, stood at 92°. On the morning of the third day they found themselves at an elevation of 4837 feet, the barometer standing 25.10, the thermometer 40°. In noting that day's experience, Lieut. Doane says:

"Throughout the forenoon it rained occasional showers, but before 12 o'clock the clouds rolled away in heavy masses along the mountain sides, the sun came out and the atmosphere was clear again. From this point a beautiful view is obtained. The mining camp of Emigrant Gulch is nearly opposite, on a small stream coming down from the mountains on the opposite side of the river. A few settlements have been made in this vicinity, and small herds of cattle range at will over the broad extent of the valley. Our camp was situated at the base of the foot-hills, near a small grove, from which flowed several large springs of clear water, capable of irrigating the whole bottom in front. The soil here is very fertile, and lies favorably for irrigation; timber is convenient, water everywhere abundant, and the climate for this region remarkably mild. Residents informed me that snow seldom fell in the valley. Stock of every kind subsist through the winter without being fed or sheltered. Excepting the Judith Basin, I have seen no district in the western territories so eligible for settlement as the upper valley of the Yellowstone. Several of the party were very successful during the morning in fishing for trout, of which we afterward had an abundant and continued supply. The Yellowstone here is from 50 to 100 yards wide, and at the lowest stage four feet deep on the riffles, running over a bed of drift boulders and gravel with a very rapid current. The flow of water is fully equal to that of the Missouri at Fort Benton, owing to the rapidity of the current, though the channel is much more narrow."

By the fifth day the party had attained an elevation of 7,331 feet, where the thermometer at noon marked 72°. Here they found themselves in the midst of indescribable volcanic wonders. They were, however, notwithstanding their great elevation, in the midst of groves of pine and aspen.

In his notes of the eighth day Lieut. Doane says:

"Barometer, 23°; thermometer, 50°; elevation, 7,270 feet.

"Coming into camp in advance, passing through a grove of pine——"

Can one who has not visited the pampas of South America, Australia, the elevated plains of Asia, or our own sheep-growing territory, imagine a forest of pines at 48° north latitude, rising from an elevation of 7,270 feet above the level of the sea?

"Coming into camp in advance, passing through a grove of pine, on the margin of a little creek, I was met face to face on the path, by two magnificent buck elk, one of which I wounded, but lost in the woods. Mr. Smith started up a small bear, which also got away. The ground was everywhere tracked by the passage of herds of elk and mountain sheep; and bear sign was everywhere visible."

The tenth day found the party at an elevation of 7,697 feet, with the thermometer at 46° in the morning. Describing the high hills, (one of which, Langford's Peak, rises abruptly to the height of 10,327 feet,) by which they were surrounded, and through which the waters of the Yellowstone poured in one of the grandest cataracts of the world, Lieut. Doane says:

"On the caps of these dizzy heights, mountain sheep and elk rest during the night. I followed down the stream on horseback, to where it breaks through the range, threading my way through the forest on game trails with little difficulty. Selecting the channel of a small creek and leaving the horses, I followed it down on foot, wading in the bed of the stream, which fell off at an angle of about 30° between walls of gypsum. Private McConnell accompanied me. On entering the ravine we came at once to hot springs of sulphur, sulphate of copper, alum, steam jets, &c., in endless variety, some of them of very peculiar form. One of them in particular of sulphur had built up a tall spire from the slope of the wall, standing out like an enormous horn, with hot water trickling down its sides. The creek ran on a bed of solid rock, in many places smooth and slippery, in others obstructed by masses of débris formed from the overhanging cliffs of the sulphuretted limestone above. After descending for three miles in the channel we came to a sort of bench or terrace, the same one seen previously in following down the creek from our first camp in the basin. Here we found a large flock of mountain sheep, very tame, and greatly astonished, no doubt, at our sudden appearance. McConnell killed one and wounded another, whereupon the rest disappeared, clambering up the steep walls with a celerity truly astonishing."

On the twelfth day, at an elevation of 7,487 feet, they discovered a recent volcano, throwing steam and mud to the height of 300 feet. I refer to this, not to dwell upon this wonder (for it was but one among a myriad), but as evidence of the condition of vegetation and the capacity of the country to sustain flocks at that elevation. Lieut. Doane says:

"The distances to which this mud has been thrown, are truly astonishing. Directly above the crater rises a steep bank, a hundred feet in height, *on the apex of which the tallest tree near is 110 feet high.* The topmost branches of this tree were loaded with mud 200 feet above and 50 feet laterally away from the crater. The ground and fallen trees near by, were splashed at a horizontal distance of 200 feet. The trees below were either broken down or their branches festooned with dry mud, which appeared in the tops of trees growing on the side hill from the same level with the crater, 50 feet in height, and at a distance of 180 feet from the volcano."

Certainly vegetation is not stunted by climate when in this elevated and volcanic region upon the apex of the hills, trees attain the height of 110 feet!

But Lieut. Doane's report is replete with evidence that the valleys are capable of sheltering sheep and cattle from the severity of climate that prevails upon the greater elevations during the winter.

But the route of the Northern Pacific Railroad is not obstructed by mountains like these; the highest point it attains being the Deer Lodge Pass through the Rocky Mountains, which is 4950 feet, being 3285 feet below the grade of the Union Pacific Road at Sherman, where, two years ago, I gathered a bouquet composed of the wild flowers common to Eastern Pennsylvania.

### *Settlements Along the Line.*

It must be admitted that a portion of the land in Dakota, Montana and Idaho, through which this road will run, is unsuited to cultivation, but the proportion is much less than will be found on the line of any more southern road. The alkali plains alone which the Union and Central road traverses are broader than the breadth of all the bad lands along the line of the Northern route. Governor Stevens, who superintended the original government survey of this line, and frequently crossed the country, said, that "not more than one-fifth of the land from Red River to Puget Sound is unsuited to cultivation, and this fifth is largely made up of mountains covered with bunch grass and valuable timber, and filled with precious metals." But, ladies and gentlemen, were it true that but one-fifth instead of four-fifths of the land granted to the Northern Pacific Company between the western boundary of Minnesota and the eastern boundary of Washington and Oregon, is presently available for the purposes of settlement, the grant would, in my judgment, be adequate for the construction of the road. Indeed, I believe that the lands granted in Minnesota, Oregon and Washington Territory, would build and equip the road.

### *Commercial Advantages.**

No part of the capital employed in constructing this road will be long un-

* The Chicago *Journal*, in an intelligent review of the Pacific Railroads, says:

The census returns of 1860 gave 460,112 as the sum total of the population of Nebraska, Wyoming, Utah, Nevada and California—the district now traversed by the Union and Central Pacific Railroads. Work was commenced on the road, at both ends, in the winter of 1863. Between the two dates mentioned, owing to the war, it is evident that the far West could not have received much of an addition to its population. Looking back now, it is easy to see why so many of its friends, even, prophesied that financially the road would be a failure. They regarded the enterprise as one of political necessity, but could see no money in it. Its route, for the most part, lay through a wilderness incapable of agricultural settlement. Of the whole number of inhabitants above given all but 90,118 were in the State of California.

* * * * *

The earnings of the Central and Union Pacific Railroad were Fourteen Millions in 1870—the net receipts over operating expenses being in excess of Six Millions. In other words, in the first year of its through business it earned enough over and above running expenses to pay six per cent. on a fair estimate of its cost. In six years the Central Pacific (forming one-half of the through line) has earned Ten Millions net, being nearly Six Millions more than the interest on its Bonds and all the the cost of operating. Sixty-five per cent. of this came from local traffic, and one year only of through business is included in it. The authorities of the Central Pacific estimate the earnings of their road for 1871 at Ten Millions, and President Thomas A. Scott, of the Union Pacific, places the earnings of that road, this year, at Nine Millions, making $19,000,000 for the through line from San Francisco to Omaha. Of this at least $9,000,000 will be net above running expenses, or 9 per cent. on a reasonable estimate of the entire cost of the road. The first mortgage bonds of the Central Pacific, bearing six per cent. interest, and secured only on the road, are now selling at 103. So oppositely to all expectation has the operation of the road turned out!

Since the commencement of the Union and Central Pacific, San Francisco has grown from being a city of sixty thousand inhabitants to be a city of a hundred and fifty thousand. But, includ-

productive, as a remunerative business awaits the completion of each section. From the Missouri at Omaha to the Sacramento no navigable stream crosses or approaches the Union and Central road, while the route of this road is traversed, at intervals of about two hundred miles, along its whole extent by navigable streams upon which there are considerable settlements. One eastern terminus of the road is the western-most point of our magnificent system of Lake navigation—the other is the head of navigation on the Mississippi river at St. Paul, a city whose population numbers about 25,000. Duluth, its lake terminus, is rising into commercial importance more rapidly than did Chicago, and with the promise of continuous growth. It is the port through which the people of Minnesota and the entire new Northwest will exchange commodities not only with all the lake ports of the U. S. and British America, but with Europe, and the commercial cities of the Atlantic seaboard. It will also be the chief outlet for the increasing tens of millions of bushels of wheat and feet of lumber, produced by the farmers and lumbermen of Minnesota. Though Duluth is not yet four years old, her foreign commerce is large enough to command the attention of the Treasury Department, and require the appointment of a deputy collector and several minor officers of customs.

---

ing that, a total population of the belt of States and Territories through which the road runs is only 788,270. And this number of people, with aid from a portion of Colorado (population 39,681) furnish business to the Union and Central Pacific at the rate of Fourteen to Nineteen Million dollars per year. This brings up the rather curious question, How many inhabitants are necessary in a given district to make a railway pay?

And now comes the Northern Pacific, certainly with greater probabilities of success than were before the Union and Central Pacific. While it equals the other in mineral wealth, the country through which it runs is vastly more inviting to the farmer. Indeed, testimony shows it to be of special agricultural value. Leaving out California on the Union-Central Pacific, and also excluding Minnesota on the Northern Pacific, and the latter road has 104,752 more people to contribute to its local business than awaited the opening of the Union and Central Pacific, and only 23,592 less than give support to the latter road now.

Including those two States, which would not be unfair, inasmuch as the Northern Pacific will have in Minnesota, with its main and branch lines, over eight hundred miles of road, draining two-thirds of the entire State—including these two States, the tributary population of the Northern road in all is 639,433, or 179,321 more than were at first reached by the Union-Central Pacific, and only 148,837 less than give aid to it now.

But the figures given are suggestive. What, principally within the last five years, has added 100,000 to the population of San Francisco? Surely nothing so much as the summons of iron knocking at the Golden Gate. If a road can add 100,000 people in five years to an existing city, cannot another one in the same time build up a city of 100,000, especially if, by reason of its shorter oceanic distance, it is demonstrated that it will necessarily control foreign shipments?

Few doubt that if the land lying along the Union Pacific had been as available for agriculture as the lands of the Northern Pacific, the population along the route would have trebled as well as that of its terminal city. Here, then, the case will probably stand:—The Northern Pacific, on its completion, will find a flourishing city awaiting it on Puget Sound, inferior, of course, in size, to San Francisco, but still a thriving, well-grown city, as helpful to it as the other to its Southern compeer. It will, during its progress, on account of its fertile lands, more than quadruple the population west of Minnesota, and so bids more than fair to equal the first through business of the Union and Central Pacific, while for the succeeding years its returns will be vastly greater.

---

### *The Northern River System.*

The settlements on the Red river of the North, the western boundary of Minnesota, are numerous, and the trade of the extended and fertile valleys it drains will await the completion of the road to that river, which will be accomplished by the 1st of September. Beyond Minnesota, the line crosses or runs upon the banks of the Dakota, Missouri and Yellowstone, which are east of the Rocky Mountains, and navigable for hundreds or thousands of miles; and beyond the Rocky Mountains, the Snake, the Cowlitz and the Columbia rivers, will prove immediate and valuable tributaries to its business. Its western termini are at Portland on the Willamette, twelve miles above its confluence with the Columbia, which is already an important commercial centre, and a point yet to be determined on the waters of Puget Sound, which are the predestined field of a commerce that, at an early day, will exceed that of San Francisco, and, in the not very distant future, equal the present commerce of New York. I cannot give the figures to show the extent of the trade of the Columbia river and its confluents, but am able to assure you from actual observation that it has been large and profitable enough to give the original stockholders of the *Oregon Steam Navigation Co.* prominent places in the roll of heavy capitalists on the Pacific Coast.

### *The Future Pacific Metropolis.*

That the commercial metropolis of the Pacific coast would be south of Puget Sound I have never believed. Observation confirmed the conviction with which Mr. Whitney had impressed me. And early in August, 1869, just after my return from the Pacific coast, at the request of Col. John W. Forney, I held a protracted conversation with Mr. Joseph I. Gilbert, an experienced phonographic reporter, who, on the 27th of that month, presented to the readers of the *Press* the substance of the interview. Recurring to the *Press* of that date, I find that, speaking on this point, I said:

"Allow me to state one conclusion from personal observation. It is that San Francisco will, in the course of time, cease to be the great city of the Pacific coast. Her location constitutes her for the present the *entrepot* for all the commerce of the coast, embracing the trade from the South American coast, from the Sandwich Islands, from China, Japan, British Columbia, and our territory north of that city. The Bay of San Francisco, too, is quite capable of accommodating the commerce of the world. It is, I think, unequalled as a bay, in extent, beauty and safety. The city has made most magnificent strides. She has her dry-dock, her ample wharves, her steam-tugs, her coast defences, and has made very considerable progress in manufactures. But notwithstanding all these advantages, my firm impression is that the great city of the Pacific coast will have its location on or near the waters of Puget Sound.

* * * * * * *

"Here are to be found in abundance timber, coal, iron, fish, wheat, all domestic grasses, the potato, apple, pear, plum, and during more than half the year, all the fruits known to our own tables. Here, in my judgment, will be located the great city of the Pacific coast, as, owing to the peculiar conformation of the Sound, communication may easily be had between distant parts of this territory by water.

"Another consideration is that a city located here would be practically nearer to China than is San Francisco; because vessels leaving San Francisco for China, notwithstanding the point for which they are destined is south of their point of departure, are compelled on account of the prevailing winds, to make what sailors call a "northing," quite up to the Straits of Fuca; in consequence of which a vessel starting from the latter point for the same destination would have an advantage of three or four days over her San Francisco competitor."

### *Some Official Testimony.*

But, ladies and gentlemen, let me hasten on and show you by official testimony the advantages presented by this route to the Pacific over any other north of the 32d parallel, on which, as I have said, the almost tropical climate would prove an obstacle to general travel and commerce. In pursuance of the act of Congress of March 3, 1853, the Topographical Engineers designated by the Secretary of War, surveyed seven routes extending from the line of the Northern Pacific southward to the 32d parallel. Their reports were referred by the Secretary of War, for examination to Captain A. A. Humphreys and Lieut. G. K. Warren, both of whom are well known to the country for the distinguished services they rendered as commanding generals during the late war, and the former of whom is now at the head of the Engineer Department of the United States Army. On the 5th of February, 1855, these officers submitted the results of their analysis and comparisons in an elaborate report, in which, speaking of the route near the 47th and 49th parallel they say:

"The advantages of this route are—its low profile, which is important in relation to climate; its easy grades, and small amount of ascents and decents, both important if the road should be developed to its full working power; the great extension west of the prairie lands; in the supplies of timber over the western half of the route; the facilities which the Columbia river and its tributaries, and the Missouri, will afford to the construction of the road; in the short distance from the Mississippi to a seaport of the Pacific; in the western terminus of the road on Puget Sound being nearer to the ports of Asia than the termini of the other routes; in the proximity of the eastern terminus to Lake Superior, from which a continuous navigation for sea-going vessels extends to the Atlantic Ocean; and in the existence of coal on Puget Sound."

The explorations had been but preliminary and had not disclosed the important fact that an abundant supply of coal is distributed at easy points along the whole route.*

On page 107 of the first volume of the report, to which I refer for a moment, is found a tabular statement, showing the relative distance by each of the seven routes surveyed; the sum of ascents and descents: the length of level route of equal working expense; the comparative cost of different routes; the number of miles of route through arable land; the number of miles of route through lands generally uncultivated, arable soil being found in small areas; number of square miles of sums of areas of largest bodies of arable land in uncultivable region; number of miles at an elevation less than 1000 feet; number at an elevation greater than 1000 and less than 2000; greater than 2000 and less than 3000; greater than 3000 and less than 4000; greater than 4000 and less than 5000; greater than 5000 and less than 6000, at which point the Northern route disappears from the table, while two of the routes have each twenty miles at grades above 10,000 feet, and both of which it would be necessary to tunnel at an elevation of 9540 feet, which is 4590 feet above the highest summit the Northern road will cross.

### *Grades—A Natural Pathway.*

In all these respects the Northern route is shown to compare favorably with all of its competitors. But its most remarkable advantage appears under the head of the sum of ascents and descents. High rates under this head indicate increased percentages of danger and current expense. The lower the rate of ascent and descent the safer and more economical is travel. And while the Northern route is charged under this head with but 19,100 feet, the route comparing most favorably with it in this respect is that on the 41st and 42d parallels, in which the sum is 29,120, an increase of more than fifty per cent.; and the extreme contrast is that of the route on the 38th and 39th parallels, in which the sum reaches 56,514.

The study of these voluminous reports will satisfy any reasonable man that from Duluth to a point on Puget Sound is nature's own route for a Pacific railroad. So startling indeed were the advantages presented by this route, that the then Secretary of War, Jefferson Davis, struck from the report of Governor Stevens, since so distinguished as a soldier and engineer, the estimate he presented of the cost, which was $117,121,000 and inserted in lieu thereof $130,781,000. His keen foresight showed him that the development of the then almost unknown Northwest, by the construction of a road upon easy gradients through a region of such wonderful resources, would, in a few years, place his beloved South and slavery at the mercy of a free people, overwhelmingly outnumbering those of the plantation States. How reckless and unjust this action was, is proven by the fact that all the more recent estimates fix the cost at but little more than sixty-six per cent. of that of Governor Stevens, or $77,000,000 for the road and original equipment.

### *Effect on American Commerce.*

The effect the completion of this road, with its immense advantages of position and grades, is to have upon our commerce cannot be predicted. I reiterate the assertion that the trade of the Pacific Ocean must find its chief *entrepot* on Puget Sound; and as evidence of my appreciation of the future extent and value of this commerce let me again refer to the remarks I made in Congress on the 26th of April, 1866. Replying to a distinguished representative

* San Francisco and her ocean steamers are now supplied with coal mined on Puget Sound, near the western terminus of the Northern Pacific Railroad. Twenty-five thousand tons were shipped for this purpose in 1870.

from Chicago, Ill., who had reminded members who were disposed to vote for aid to the Northern Pacific Road, that a Congressional election was at hand, I said:

"I appeal from the constituents of the gentleman from Chicago [Mr. Wentworth], on the eve of an election, to posterity, and ask gentlemen to view the proposed enterprise in the light in which future generations will behold it. They will look beyond the vast and undeveloped empire I have indicated; for beyond it lies the broad Pacific, capable of bearing a commerce a thousand times heavier than has ever chafed the waters of the Atlantic, but on which our flag is seen floating only from the masts of coasting craft or whalers wending their slow way to the Northern seas in quest of hard-earned wealth. So slight is our power upon this ocean that the recently pardoned rebel Semmes, with a single vessel, destroyed nearly a hundred of our peaceable whalers, giving their cargoes, gathered by years of dangerous toil, to the flames or the waves. It bounds our country for more than a thousand miles, and our maritime power, which could not now protect a mile of it, should be seen and felt upon it, and our flag and white sails or the curling smoke of our steamers should shadow its every wave.

"The commerce of the Pacific ocean belongs to us; and we should confirm our title by the right of occupancy; for when we cast our eyes beyond its placid surface, we behold what is to be our next conquest. The Old World is to be awakened by American ideas. Its unnumbered people are to be quickened, instructed, and redeemed by American enterprise. Some statisticians tell us that there are 750,000,000 people in the ancient theocratic countries of the East, which is the West to which the star of our commercial empire will next take its way. Others put the population at 1,000,000,000; and others at 1,300,000,000. There, where civilization dawned and the drowsy past yet lingers, the first impulses of a new cycle begin to be felt. Japan is yielding to the impulses of our age. The Chinese wall is crumbling away. It was but yesterday that I had a letter informing me that our countryman, Dr. Martin, interpreter of the American Legation at Pekin, under the employment of the Chinese Government, had rendered into that language our Wheaton's Law of Nations. Thus, that vast and long isolated Power is preparing to enter into commercial connections with the world. The ancient civilization of Asia is giving way, the doctrine of sacred castes is about to yield to the sublimer creed of man's freedom and equality. Muscular labor will soon be done there by the potent agents we now employ—coal and iron—and the genius of the buried dead, embodied in mechanism, will soon relieve their toiling millions as it now does ours. Their whole life is to be quickened by modern enterprise, and they will swell the numbers of the people on our Pacific slope."

When it is asserted that these roads will give us the control of the commerce of China, purblind philosophers point to the small portion of that trade carried by the Central and Union road as proof that that commerce will never cross our country. It is not two years since that road was completed. Commerce follows cheap and rapid lines of transit, and railroad fares are regulated by the amount of business done. Thus in 1850, by the average rate of fares on American roads, it cost $20 to transport a ton of wheat 100 miles; in 1870, a ton of wheat was transported the same distance for $1.25. [Applause.] With increase of business the Central and Union Pacific Road will be able, while increasing its profits, to reduce its rates for freight and travel. It is doing it already. Its present rates for passengers and freight compare, as I have said, most favorably with those of 1869; and when twenty or thirty other branches, like those to Denver and Salt Lake City, shall throw their business upon the trunk line, and when other Evanstons and Cheyennes shall have sprung up, when Omaha shall be a city like San Francisco, and San Francisco a city like Philadelphia, all which may occur within the next quarter of a century, who shall say how small will be the charge for carrying a chest of tea or a case of silk? It will be very small, and when railroads shall be able to carry this freight as cheaply and more quickly than it can be moved by steamers, the trade of China and Japan will cross our continent, and my prophecies of 1846 and 1850 will be more than fulfilled, as the Pennsylvania road will carry the freight of two Pacific roads—one from San Francisco and the other from the Columbia and Puget Sound. [Applause.]

### *Pacific Coast Harbors.—Puget Sound.*

Among the strange contrasts presented by our two coasts, few are more impressive than the coast line itself. Harbors are numerous along the Atlantic coast. No seaboard State is without one or more good harbors. Count them, from Galveston northward and eastward to Portland, Maine, and the number will surprise you. The agricultural and mineral productions of almost every State could be floated to the sea, while our long Pacific coast, south of Alaska, presents but four harbors or fair points for commercial centres, the Bays of San Diego and San Francisco, the Columbia River and Puget Sound, the entrance to which is the Straits of Fuca. The Alleghanies are inland mountains; but the "coast range," as their name indicates, lie along the coast of the Pacific, leaving harbors only where the great waters have forced their way through the rocks.

As I have said, the commerce of China and Japan must near our coast north of the Bay of San Francisco, north even of the mouth of the Columbia, and at a point near to the Straits of Fuca. While, therefore, the commerce of the Pacific must to some extent be shared by San Diego, San Francisco, Portland, and Astoria, a city yet to arise on Puget Sound will be its great centre.

*Productions, Resources and Seasons.*

Would that I could convey to your minds a moderate conception of the wealth and climate of this far Northwestern country and of the body of water called the Straits of Fuca and Puget Sound—so calm, so deep, so guarded by forests such as no man who has not visited them has ever seen. The Straits of Fuca run in an almost direct course more than ninety miles, at an average width of more than ten miles. The shore-line of Puget Sound is nearly 1900 miles, but, such is its conformation, that the points at greatest distance from each other are not four hundred miles apart. The Sound is a series of canals, bays, inlets and harbors. Gov. Stevens, who lived on its shores for a number of years, likened it to a tree, with a very recognizable body called Admiralty Inlet, and innumerable side-branches, the trunk and branches filling a region seventy nautical miles in length from north to south, and thirty in breadth from east to west. In speaking of it again, he said:

"On the whole west coast, from San Diego to the north, nothing like this is met. All the water channels of which Admiralty inlet is composed, are comparatively narrow and long. They have more or less bold shores and are throughout very deep and abrupt, so much so that in many places a ship's side will strike the shore before the keel will touch the ground. Even in the interior and hidden parts, depths of 50 and 100 fathoms occur as broad as De Fuca Strait itself. Vancouver found 60 fathoms near the Vashon Island within a cable length of the shore, and in Possession Sound he found no soundings with a line of 110 fathoms. Our modern, more extensive soundings prove that this depth diminishes toward the extremities of the inlets and basins. Nothing can exceed the beauty and safety of these waters for navigation. Not a shoal exists within them; not a hidden rock; no sudden overfalls of the water or the air; no such strong flaws of the wind as in other narrow waters, for instance as in those of Magellan's Straits. And there are in this region so many excellent and most secure ports that the commercial marine of the Pacific ocean may be here easily accommodated."

There is but little waste land in Oregon and Washington Territory. Oregon embraces 60,975,360 acres, and its population in 1870 was but 90,933. Washington Territory contains 112,730,240 acres, and the census takers found but 23,955 civilized people dwelling upon them. This State and Territory are among the most fertile and productive sections of our country. The wheat of Oregon and Washington, as you may ascertain by consulting the commercial papers of San Francisco, commands, in the markets of that city, ten cents per bushel more than the wheat of California; and oats from the Territory are worth fifteen cents per cental more than the best California oats. As we get the wheat of the entire Pacific slope through California, we know it only as California wheat; but in the home market the difference I have indicated is constantly maintained by reason of the superiority of the more northern grain.

The forests that shelter these waters are composed of trees running up from 250 to 350 feet, with a diameter of from 8 to 12 feet, and throwing out their first arms at from 60 to 100 feet above the ground. In these glorious solitudes, upon the waters of Puget Sound there are in operation saw mills that will this year ship largely over 200,000,000 feet of superior lumber to San Francisco, Callao, Valparaiso, the Sandwich Islands, Australia and China. These forests, an inexhaustible store of wealth in themselves, are underlaid by rich deposits of coal, iron, gold and silver. The beds of iron and coal are already utilized to some extent; and the existence of the precious metals, is established by the fact that the washings of the water-courses furnish traces of gold and other metals. Of the fish with which these waters teem, I dare not tax your credulity by speaking.

Though bounded by the 49th degree of latitude, the climate is genial throughout the year. So mild are the winters—indeed, I may say, so free is the country from winter—that, notwithstanding the moisture of the climate, west of the Coast range, no provision is made for housing cattle at any season of the year. In the month of July, 1869, within the limits of Astor's old fort, near the mouth of the Columbia river, I picked from the orchard of a farmer who had gone thither from Bedford County, Pa., a variety of delicious apples, pears and plums; and from vines near the trunks of the trees, raspberries, strawberries and blackberries—a combination of fruits that could not be found in the month of July upon the best cultivated and most fortunately situated farm in Pennsylvania. And a week before, our party had found Indian women and children vending these fruits and the apricot in the streets of Victoria, the capital of British Columbia.

At Olympia, the capital of Washington Territory, situated at the head of Puget Sound, it was my pleasure to pass the greater part of a day with my young friend Elwood Evans, Esq., son of Chas. Evans, the press manufacturer of this city (whom I recognize among my auditors), and to gather luscious fruit from tree and vine in the gardens attached to his comfortable home and his law-office hard by upon the same street.

### *The Work of Development.*

Do you ask, as others have done, why with such stores of wealth, waiting to respond with such boundless generosity to the demands of man, the population does not equal one man, woman or child, to each square mile? If you do, the answer is ready. It is because the people and Government of the United States did not promptly respond to the suggestion of Asa Whitney, and either by the means proposed by him, or those they should select connect our Pacific territory with the great lakes by a railway. Had that been done, and the way been then opened to emigrants, Washington Territory would long since have been divided into two or more States, California and Oregon would be great commercial rivals, and the population of our Pacific States would equal or exceed that of busy and blessed New England.

To reach the golden lands of the Pacific coast has been a matter of too much time and expense for the poor man, and too full of trials for families. The fact that in spite of these almost insuperable difficulties, so many intelligent people have found their way thither is a testimonial to the wonderful attractions of the country, and the immense rewards it offers to industry and enterprise.

Build this road, open these multiform and exhaustless resources to the poor but enterprising people of the Eastern States and Europe, and population will flow into them so rapidly that they who shall a few years hence hear the story of the doubts of to-day about the Northern Pacific Railroad will experience wonder similar to that which you feel at the want of forecast that characterized the people of Pennsylvania twenty-five years ago, when they shrank from embarking so small a percentage of their capital in building the Pennsylvania Central road; and in a few years the trunk line of this great thoroughfare will carry the trade of innumerable lateral branches, penetrating not only our valleys but those of the British Colonies to the North, whose people will thus be made tributary to us forever, or induced to unite their destinies with ours, under a common constitution and flag. This is not declamation or prophecy. It is the announcement of conclusions that flow irresistibly from an ample store of unquestioned facts.

Do you ask whence the population would have come to effect the changes I have indicated? By the construction of the road, the character of the climate and resources of the country would have been disclosed long years ago, and the sheep-growers of the States from Vermont to Iowa would have transferred their flocks to the Asiatic and Australian fields that slope the Rocky Mountains. The hardy lumbermen from the forests of New England and northern Pennsylvania would have found their way to these richer forests in more genial climes. Nor would we then have suffered the decline in our ship-building so much and so justly bemoaned; for difficult of access as the country is, and slender as is its population and commerce, we found along these woody shores ship-yards, having on the stocks first-class ships, the outer planks of which were without a joint, having been cut sheer from one of the monarchs of the forest on the shores of the Sound. The increased coast trade of the Pacific commerce between our Atlantic and Pacific ports would have kept alive this decaying branch of business, which with the completion of the Northern Pacific Railroad, must revive with grander proportions than it ever assumed in the past.

Where will the people come from to make this wealth available, to build cities at the points along this road at which railroad and river traffic shall intersect, to raise provisions for the mining camps, and to build up commerce on Puget Sound and the Columbia river? What American, whose memory is good for a quarter of a century, asks this question? Where have the people come from who, since we discussed the propriety of building the Pennsylvania Railroad, and Asa Whitney submitted the project of a Pacific road, have settled Iowa and Wisconsin, whose joint population, though then but 200,000, now numbers two millions and a quarter, each having over a million? Where did the people come from who, within a brief quarter of a century have doubled the population of the Northern States of the Union? Where have the people come from who have meanwhile populated so many of the gold and silver-producing sections of our vast territories, and built up the States of Texas, California, Minnesota and Oregon? Let Edward Young, Esq., Chief of the Bureau of Statistics, answer these questions. I hold in my hand a recent report of his—a document that should be circulated by millions through the Eastern States and Europe. It is entitled, "Special Report on Immigration, accompanying Information for Immigrants relative to the Prices and Rentals of Lands, the Staple Products, Facilities of Access to Market, Cost of Farm Stock, Kind of Labor in Demand in the Western and Southern States, etc." This report shows that during the 8 years terminating with the 31st of December, 1846, we received 736,887 immigrants, of whom 416,950 came from the British Isles. But, Mr. Doubter, you interrupt me to ask whether this tide of immigration will continue? whether it has not reached its climax? The Chief of the Bureau of Statistics shall answer you again; for his report shows that during the like period of 8 years, terminating the 31st of last December, we received 2,307,554 immigrants, of whom there came from the British Isles 1,015,517, or more than 33 per cent., more than the entire immigration during the former eight years.

Yes, the tide of immigration will continue, and for many years it will increase. Each year will see its volume rolling in, until regenerated Europe shall give the laborer political power and social consideration. [Applause.] Our cheap land

and democratic institutions will bring her bone and sinew and enterprise to develop the resources and add to the wealth and power of our country. [Loud applause.] And nothing will do more to promote the movement than the advertisement to all the world of the vast resources of the region through which this road is to run and the wonderful field for labor, enterprise and adventure at its Pacific termini.*

### *Philadelphia Interests.*

But what will be the effect of the road upon Philadelphia? What relations has all this to our city and State? These questions which you propounded to me in your invitation, have, I think, been answered by what I have said. What State or city shares more largely than ours in the general prosperity or depression of the country? Who will be more benefited by the cheapening of freight on raw materials and manufactured articles than we? What American city produces so many of the comforts and luxuries which the people along the line of this road will consume as Philadelphia? Their demands will stimulate our industry, and their abounding means will enable them to reward it abundantly. The construction of one railroad bridge—that over the Mississippi river at St. Louis—gave to one Philadelphia firm, the Wm. Butcher Steel Works, a contract for $500,000 worth of steel. And even now, hundreds of Philadelphia mechanics are busy building locomotives and passenger and freight cars for the Northern Pacific Railroad.

I need not elaborate this point. We are a community of working people. The mass of the citizens of Philadelphia absolutely live by manual labor. The prosperity of the capitalists of this city is dependent upon the steady employment and liberal wages of her working people. [Applause.] When labor is idle, capital is idle, or employed at little profit; when the laborer earns no wages, the landlord is not always sure of his rent. [Laughter and applause.] The effect that the construction of this road will have upon the employment and wages of laboring people was discussed by me in the Congressional remarks to which I have already referred. Let me read a paragraph or two from what I then said:

"But the inviting field of the ocean, and the vast field of enterprise and reward open to us in Asia are not the only considerations that induce me to support this bill. The laboring people of every eastern city have an intense interest in this question. The safety of our country depends upon the intelligence, the virtue, the stability of our laboring people. He legislates not wisely for a democratic republic who does not make it the aim of all his acts to improve the material condition of the great laboring masses of the country. If we would perpetuate our institutions, we must see that the wages of labor are so maintained that the children of the laboring man shall grow up amid the endearments of home, and with the expectation that their children shall find more elegance and refinement in their homes than their parents were familiar with in childhood.

"The construction of a road through our northern gold region will open a field that will be a constant refuge for the surplus labor of our eastern States. There will be a refuge for those masses of ingenious workmen who are jostled each year by lack of adjustment of their numbers to the demand for their branch of labor, or are deprived of the advantage of the skill they acquired in youth by the invention of labor-saving machinery; and instead of finding themselves, as age gathers on their brow, without the means of livelihood, rich fields of enterprise, easily reached, will cheer their declining years.

"But again, the depression of our laboring people springs not alone or chiefly from local causes. Beyond the Atlantic Ocean there are 250,000,000

* A late number of the St. Paul *Pioneer*, speaking of the tide of population already pouring to the line of the Northern Pacific Railroad, says:—

"The roads leading to the Red River Valley are literally covered with emigrant wagons, with their usual accompaniment of families, furniture, and stock of all kinds. The wagon roads from Sauk Centre to St. Peter show daily accessions to the vast caravan wending its way to the fertile regions of Northern Minnesota. The extent of the great incoming tide of humanity can be best estimated on the main road between Alexandria and Pomme de Terre. Two hundred wagons per day pass over this portion of the route northwest, and the camp fires are seldom allowed to go out—a fresh train of emigrants arrives almost as soon as its predecessor has resumed its march. A noticeable feature of this year's emigration is its quality—the wagons come loaded with household goods and farming implements, and are followed by herds of cattle and other stock which in quality would do credit to any country."

people, in every community of which laboring men are held as raw material; and under the grasping influence of capital, and the oppression of despotic government are held in such bondage, that they are made to subsist, even when they toil most assiduously, upon a modicum of the elements of life, upon a minimum of the amount that will keep the soul in a tolerably sound body. Escaping from this subjection, they are borne to our shores by tens and hundreds of thousands each year. They are strangers in a strange land, many of them unacquainted with our language and habits, and are unconsciously and unwillingly the means of depressing wages. But if we give to the company the means to inaugurate work on this road, we will not only relieve the laboring masses of our crowded eastern cities, but furnish employment for more than the annual influx of those whom we gladly welcome, because they strengthen and enrich us by their toil. Could we drain Europe of its surplus laborers we would raise her wages as she now too often depresses ours.

"What will be the true policy of the builders of this road? Will it not be to employ as laborers, the heads of families, and to pay them with land and money, and settle the families along the line of the road, so that the laborer of one year will, in the next, farm his land and supply fresh laborers with bread? Thus will he who enters into an engagement with the company a pauper, or little better, find himself at the end of a year or two an independent farmer upon the world's great commercial highway. The managers of the road must pursue this policy, and will thus create business for and guard their road; thus, too, they will quicken the mineral and agricultural resources of the country, and give to the tax collector, whether at a port of entry, or in the service of the internal revenue department, more money each year than this bill is likely to cause to be taken from the treasury."

"I ask gentlemen in considering this question to rise to its dignity and grandeur. I am, sir, a devotee to freedom, but would make every country in the world tributary to my own. I delight in every manifestation of my country's power, and glow with pride as I contemplate its gigantic proportions, and see how rapidly its people subdue the wilderness, and would, as I have said, make every nation tributary to its power; but I would do this, not by oppressing any people, not by war with any government, but by improving the condition of the masses of my countrymen and those who may become such by emigration, and showing the rulers and people of the world how speedily free institutions exalt the poor and oppressed of all nations into free, self-sustaining and self-governing citizens. It is in our power to do this, and by no other means can we do it so well or quickly as by passing this supplement and vivifying the charter granted to the Northern Pacific Railroad Company."

But, ladies and gentlemen, I have detained you too long, and must close. Not, however, until I shall have reminded you that the grades and snows of the Alleghanies have not interfered with the prosperity of the Pennsylvania Railroad Company. That road has not been a failure. It has done something for the improvement of Philadelphia. It is the most profitable railroad, and most powerful corporation in the United States. [Applause.] It has stretched its controlling influence clear across the Continent. Its vice-president, our esteemed townsman, Thomas A. Scott, Esq., is the master-spirit of the Union Pacific Company, and of more than one line connecting it with Philadelphia. [Applause.] Roads owned or managed by the Pennsylvania Company await the business of the Northern Pacific road, both at St. Paul and Duluth. It has built a road to Erie, our beautiful city of the Lakes, where vessels charged with freight at Duluth will in the early spring and later autumn of each year, discharge cargo for New York and Boston, and throughout the season of Lake navigation, for Philadelphia and Baltimore; and it requires but little power of the imagination to behold Erie expanding into generous rivalry with Buffalo, Cleveland and Detroit.

Though the great characteristics of Philadelphia will always be those of a manufacturing city, her commerce is to revive. She will have not *a* line but numerous lines of steamships; and many of the men who now hear me will see the day when her existing wharf line will be wholly inadequate for her commerce. Indeed the completion of the Northern Pacific road, with the steadily increasing trade of the Central route will settle the now vexed question of a railroad along the entire river front, and require the construction of docks from Greenwich Point to Richmond. But familiar as you are with the resources of our city and State, and the advanced condition of our industries, I leave you to estimate the impulse that will be given to every interest and industry of our people by the early completion of the Northern Pacific Railroad. [Amid earnest and prolonged applause the speaker retired.]

# Climate and Resources of Montana.

By B. F. POTTS,

GOVERNOR OF MONTANA TERRITORY.

In the middle of the continent, between the Great Lakes and the Pacific Ocean—in the heart of that New Northwest, the extent, character and resources of which the people are at last beginning to appreciate—embracing within its boundaries four parallels of latitude and no less than twelve degrees of longitude, lies the great Territory of Montana. The superficial area of this territory is extensive enough to make three states as large as New York, the Empire State of the East; and, as I have stated elsewhere, I believe it to be the richest region in agricultural and mineral resources on the American continent. There are at least fifty thousand square miles of tillable land within its limits; and this land, under a cheap and simple process of irrigation, is of unsurpassed fertility, yielding in the greatest abundance all varieties of the cereals. I have seen samples of wheat which yielded eighty bushels to the acre, and the average yield, even with the very imperfect methods of cultivation which are in vogue here, is from forty to sixty-five bushels. This exceeds the yield of the famous wheat-fields of Minnesota, and is about four times as great as the average wheat crop of Ohio. Rye, oats and barley produce enormously, and the yield of vegetables is simply without a parallel in the history of horticulture in America. The common yield of potatoes, for instance, is 400 bushels per acre.

Lands for grazing purposes, too, are of vast extent and of the best quality. Grasses as nutritious as sheaf-oats cover the hills and valleys and extend far up the mountain sides, affording pasturage for numberless herds of cattle and sheep during the entire year. The cattle alone now to be found in the Territory number at least sixty thousand head, and so abundant are these grasses, and so mild is our climate, that no grain or hay is fed to them at all—they take care of themselves and keep fat all winter. Our meat markets are supplied with beef taken from among the different herds at all seasons of the year, and it is found to be of the fattest and sweetest, making delicious food, superior generally in quality and flavor to the grain fed stock of the States. Certainly no country can surpass this for grazing purposes; and there is none where, in the future, when the Northern Pacific Railroad has reached us, such fortunes are to be made in the business of raising stock for the market.

Of the mineral wealth of Montana all the world has heard. Not less than twelve million dollars' worth of gold-dust was taken from the mines last season, and iron, copper, coal, and other minerals exist in exhaustless abundance.

I suppose, however, that the thing about our New Northwest which has most surprised the public is the genial character of its climate. Radically different as it may seem from the prevalent idea regarding it, it is nevertheless true that the climate of Montana, as a whole, is milder than that of New York, while the purity and dryness of the atmosphere make the variations of temperature far less noticeable. The old theory that the further north we go the more severe the climate becomes is now generally exploded. It is understood, at last, that isothermal divisions, except in their larger aspects, are entirely independent of degrees of latitude; and the various explorers and topographers who have been sent out here by the Government have shown by instrumental tests that the temperature of Walla Walla, on the 46th degree of latitude, is the same as that of Washington City, on the 38th; that of Clark's Fork, in Montana, on the 48th, the same as that of St. Joseph, Missouri, on the 41st; and that of the Bitter Root Valley, Missoula County, Montana, on the 46th, the same as that of Philadelphia, on the 41st.

The winters in this section are generally open and pleasant, as may be inferred from the fact of the cattle grazing without shelter all winter. The valleys are hardly ever covered with snow, and it is rare that the roads are not dry and passable for ten months in the year. On the mountains, of course, as in moutainous regions usually, winter sometimes pinches hard, and snow falls to considerable depths; but even the mountains are not the least attractive features of the territory. The elevation of the mountains, valleys, and plains of Montana above the level of the sea is from 2,000 to 4,000 feet less than that of Wyoming and Utah. This fact alone goes far to explain the milder climate and vastly greater productiveness of Montana.

How this great wealth, agricultural and mineral, is to be utilized and made to contribute its due share to the nation's commercial prosperity is a question not less important to the people at large than to the inhabitants of Montana itself; and in considering it I am brought to that great enterprise, the Northern Pacific Railroad, now building and destined to traverse from east to west our entire territory. This road will drain our richest valleys, and furnish an outlet for the immense future surplus productions of the Territory. All that has heretofore been written about the superior land-grant of the Northern Pacific Railroad in Montana, scarcely gives an adequate conception of the extent and true value of the grant. The company will receive twenty-five thousand six hundred acres of our best agricultural and grazing land for every mile of road that is built—lands which not only possess all the advantages which I have mentioned, but are within easy reach of timber, and abound in fine building-stone of almost every variety and inexhaustible in quantity. I have no doubt that these lands will not only cancel the entire cost of building the railroad, but will leave a surplus to the company.

The Northern Pacific Railroad is of immense importance to Montana. It will enable our stock raisers to compete on favorable terms with those of Illinois and other states in the markets of the Eastern cities. A new impetus will be given to all our industries. Our mines will be developed, new ones will be opened, and those that produced twelve million dollars in gold last season will far exceed that sum annually. Our population will rapidly increase: the sixty-two cities and towns we now have will be doubled in number and quadrupled in size; and the public land, now unoccupied, will be cultivated by actual settlers. Other prosperous states will spring up around us; and before we enter upon another decade this great Northwest, now lying broad and inviting before the settler, will be contributing its rightful share toward the wealth, commerce, and general prosperity of the nation.

The enterprise which is opening this New Northwest is truly a great national work, and well deserves the encouragement, co-operation and support alike of all who, as Americans, feel an interest in the country's progress, or who as capitalists desire a liberal return upon investment.

www.ingramcontent.com/pod-product-compliance
Lightning Source LLC
LaVergne TN
LVHW011134110826
845150LV00008B/2335

* 9 7 8 1 4 1 8 1 9 3 9 3 5 *